Aberdeenshire

C O U N C I L

Aberdeenshire Libraries
www.aberdeenshire.gov.uk/libraries
Renewals Hotline 01224 661511

Aberdeenshire

REPTILES

BookLife

GRACE JONES

Words that appear like **this** can be found in the glossary on page 24.

©2017
Book Life
King's Lynn
Norfolk PE30 4LS

ISBN: 978-1-78637-032-7

Written by:
Grace Jones

Designed by:
Matt Rumbelow

A catalogue record for this book
is available from the British Library.

Contents

What are Living Things?

All living things move and grow. Living things need air, food, water and sunlight to stay alive.

These are all living things.

Frog

Tiger

Human

4

Knife,
Fork &
Plate

Books

These are all
non-living
things.

Non-living things do not move or grow. Non-living things do not need air, food, water or sunlight because they are not alive.

Teddy Bear

5

What is a Reptile?

Reptiles are living things that can live in water and on land. They need air, food, water and sunlight to live. Lizards, tortoises and crocodiles are all types of reptile.

Lizard

Tortoise

Crocodile

Reptiles have **scales** all over their bodies, have backbones and usually lay their eggs on land. They are also cold-blooded animals. This means that their body temperature changes when the temperature outside gets hotter or colder.

Fact: There are over **9,500** known species of reptile.

Scales

Eggs

Where do they Live?

All living things live in a **habitat** or home. Some reptiles live near to or in water, including in rainforests, oceans and rivers.

Other reptiles live on dry land,
in the deserts, mountains and
grasslands found on planet Earth.

Reptile Homes

Reptiles can live in many different habitats found around the world. A common habitat for snakes is under the ground in a cave or a nest. Their underground homes provide them with shelter from **predators** and a safe place to hide their eggs.

Viper Nest

Some reptiles live in very hot **climates**, such as desert habitats, which get very little rain every year. Reptiles, such as lizards, can live on little water and try to keep themselves out of the sun's heat as much as possible.

Desert Spiny Lizard

What do they Eat?

Most reptiles are **carnivores**. They eat small animals, such as birds, mice and fish. Snakes and crocodiles are known to eat much larger **prey**, such as deer, buffalo and zebra.

Fact:
Some reptiles don't need to drink any water because they absorb it through their skin.

Most reptiles have large jaws and swallow their prey whole rather than chewing it. It can take as long as six months for some snakes to **digest** their food!

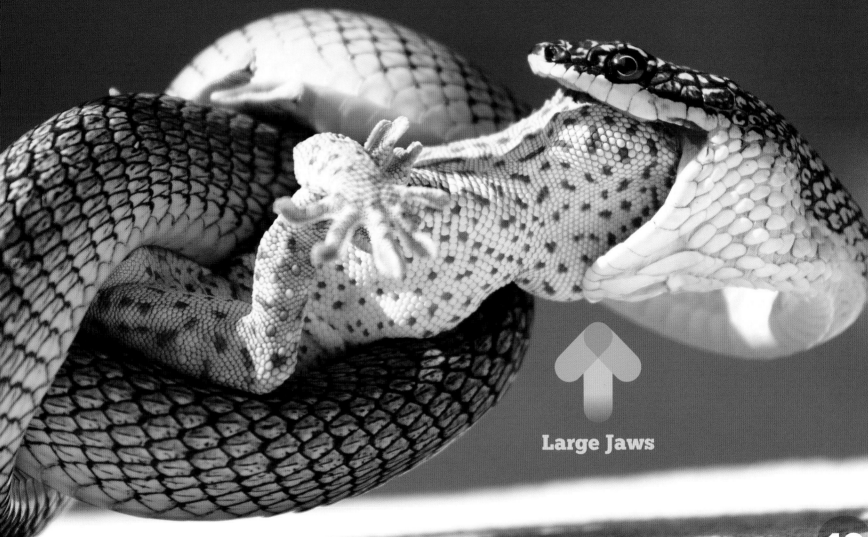

Large Jaws

How do they Breathe?

All reptiles breathe oxygen from the air through their two lungs. Reptiles move the muscles in-between their ribs and stomach to breathe in and out.

Fact: Some snake species breathe through only one lung.

Some species of turtle are able to breathe underwater. The Common Musk turtle is able to take in air underwater because it can absorb oxygenin the water through its tongue.

The Common Musk turtle is found in the freshwater lakes and rivers of North America.

How do they Move?

Most reptiles use their strong legs to help them to move their bodies. Crocodiles use their tails to help them swim, whilst some lizards can shed their tails to help them run away from predators.

A lizard who has shed its tail.

Reptiles without legs, such as snakes, use bones called ribs and muscles to help to move themselves along the ground. They also use their scales to help them to grip the ground as they are moving.

Snake Bones

Muscles

Scales

How do they Grow?

Most reptiles start life inside their mothers' eggs before they are ready to **hatch**. They usually cut through their eggshells with their teeth or break them using their bodies. Other reptiles, including some snakes and lizards, give birth to live young.

After they hatch, some reptile parents continue to look after and feed their young. Their young continue to grow and change until they are fully grown adults. This can take anywhere from a few weeks to more than thirty years for some species of tortoise.

Galapagos Tortoise

Remarkable Reptiles

Reptiles can be very colourful. The Panther chameleon lives in the rainforests of Madagascar and can change colour to red or yellow when it is angry.

Some lizards have found clever ways to scare their predators. The Frill-Necked lizard from Australia fans out the skin around its neck to frighten other animals.

World Record Breakers

SALTWATER CROCODILE

Record: The World's Biggest Reptile!

Size: Up to 6 metres long

Fact: A group of crocodiles is called a 'congregation'.

Fact: Saltwater crocodiles live in the rivers and creeks of **Australia** and live for up to 70 years.

DIMORPHODON

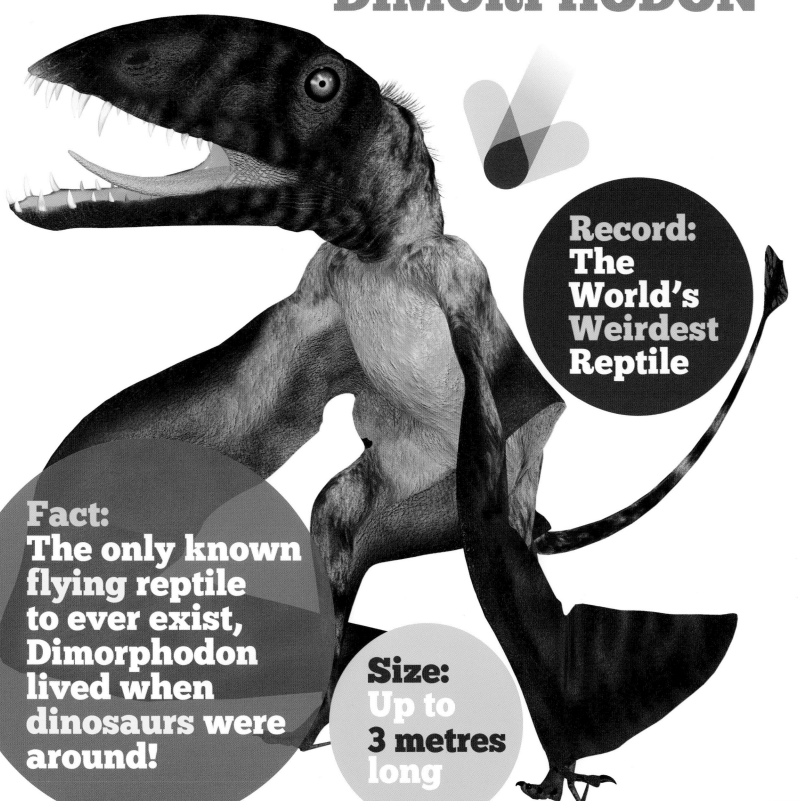

Record:
The World's Weirdest Reptile

Fact:
The only known flying reptile to ever exist, Dimorphodon lived when dinosaurs were around!

Size:
Up to 3 metres long

Glossary

carnivores animals that feed on other animals rather than plants

climates types of weather in a particular place

digest to break down food into things that can be used by the body

habitat a home where animals and plants live

hatch when young come out of an egg

predators animals that eat other animals and insects.

prey any animal that is hunted by another

scales small circles of thin bone that protect the skin of fish and reptiles

Index

Photo Credits

Abbreviations: l-left, r-right, b-bottom, t-top, c-centre, m-middle.
Front Cover: TheLightPainter, 1 - Kuttelvaserova Stuchelova, 2/3 – reptiles4all, 4bl – Chros. 4c – Eric Isselee. 4r – michaeljung. 5bl – Elena Schweitzer. 5tl – koosen. 5r – Lichtmeister. 6t – Olga_Serova, 6m - Svetoslav Radkov, 6b – nattanan726, 7 - Heiko Kiera, 8 - Attila JANDI, 9 - Janelle Lugge, 10 – dmitriyGo, 11 - Amy Nichole Harris, 12 - Kuttelvaserova Stuchelova, 13 – Trahcus, 14 – nattanan726, 15 - Marek Velechovsky, 16 - Matt Jeppson, 17t – bluehand, 17b - Graphic Compressor, 18 - Trevor kelly, 19 - ANDRZEJ GRZEGORCZYK, 20 - Arto Hakola, 21 - Eric Isselee, 22 - Volodymyr Burdiak, 23 – Catmando. Images are courtesy of Shutterstock.com. With thanks to Getty Images, Thinkstock Photo and iStockphoto.